CW01468708

Original title:
Celestial Metamorphosis

Author: Eliora Lumiste
ISBN HARDBACK: 978-1-80561-232-2
ISBN PAPERBACK: 978-1-80561-793-8

From Dust to Light

In shadows deep, we find our spark,
A whisper soft, ignites the dark.
From grain to glow, we rise anew,
Embracing hope, like morning dew.

With every step, we shed our past,
In fleeting time, our dreams are cast.
The weight we bear transforms to flight,
From humble dust, we soar to light.

The journey winds through valleys low,
Each trial faced, a chance to grow.
In unity, our voices blend,
From ashes born, our souls transcend.

The path unfolds, horizons wide,
Where courage dwells, and fears subside.
From dust to light, we weave our tale,
In endless love, we'll never fail.

Through darkest nights, we hold on tight,
For every end, begets a light.
With hearts ablaze, we greet the dawn,
From dust to light, we'll carry on.

Eclipsed Whispers

In shadows thick, a silence grows,
A murmured tale that no one knows.
The light retreats, a gentle sigh,
As dreams dissolve in twilight sky.

Soft echoes dance, a fleeting thrill,
In twilight's hush, the heart stands still.
A secret held in twilight's palm,
The world transforms, so soft, so calm.

Beneath a cloak of starry mist,
The whispers weave through twilight's twist.
Each heartbeat sings a hidden song,
In eclipsed realms where shadows throng.

Yet in this dark, a spark ignites,
A glimmering hope through endless nights.
When darkness falls, the stars align,
Through whispered dreams, the light will shine.

Astral Crossroads

At the crossroads where dreams convene,
The paths of fate, both bright and keen.
In the starlit night, choices arise,
Guided by whispers of endless skies.

One road of light, another of shade,
In each direction, memories made.
With every step, our hearts align,
In the astral glow, destinies shine.

The map is drawn in stardust trails,
Each decision spins its own tales.
Navigating through the cosmic dance,
Together we forge our timeless chance.

In moments of doubt, look to the sky,
For stars will guide us, we will not shy.
The crossroads hold both joy and pain,
In unity we rise, in love we gain.

With open hearts, we choose our way,
Through the astral night, we boldly sway.
Together we stand, come what may,
In the dance of worlds, we find our stay.

The Symphony of Stars

Each twinkling light, a note of grace,
In infinite space, they find their place.
With every glance, a story told,
The symphony of stars, forever bold.

Voices of cosmos, softly sing,
Echoing truths that time can bring.
A celestial concert for all to hear,
Notes filled with joy, longing, and fear.

As constellations guide our way,
We journey forth, night turns to day.
The beauty found in endless skies,
Reminds us always to dream and rise.

In every star, a wish ignites,
A promise of peace in darkest nights.
Together we weave our dreams so near,
In the symphony, we shall persevere.

United in harmony, we play our part,
As dreamers and seekers, we feel the art.
A cosmic dance, forever ours,
The symphony of endless stars.

Nightfall Transformations

When the sun dips low, shadows grow,
A canvas of stars begins to show.
In the twilight's kiss, magic brews,
Whispers of dreams in vibrant hues.

The moonlight dances on silver streams,
Awakening wonders, weaving dreams.
Each night transforms the world we know,
A symphony of darkness, softly aglow.

In quiet corners, secrets unfold,
Tales of the brave and stories bold.
Night cloaks the fears we cannot face,
Fostering hope in the darkness' embrace.

Beneath the stars, we find our place,
Each constellation, a timeless trace.
Night's gentle hand guides us to see,
The transformations of what can be.

As dawn approaches, the magic wanes,
Yet in our hearts, the night remains.
A journey crafted in shadows long,
In nightfall's arms, we find our song.

The Convergence of Light

In dawn's embrace, shadows depart,
A dance of colors in the heart.
Golden beams stretch across the sky,
Whispers of hope, as day draws nigh.

Each ray connects the dreams we share,
A tapestry woven, vibrant and rare.
The sun ascends, casting its net,
Volatile moments we shall not forget.

Through morning's mist, the world awakes,
A symphony played by nature's stakes.
In every glimmer, life ignites,
The convergence of all our lights.

With every step, the path unfolds,
Stories of courage, quietly told.
In the warmth of a shared embrace,
We find our truth in this sacred space.

Together we rise, hand in hand,
Building a future, bold and grand.
The dawn of unity shines bright,
As we embrace the convergence of light.

A Symphony of Shifting Light

Eons before, they forged their own fate,
In the quiet of darkness, they resonate.
Colors transition, creating pure art,
A symphony of light that sings to the heart.

From red giants blazing to white dwarfs so meek,
Their harmony whispers, the ancients all speak.
In the pulse of the cosmos, a rhythm takes flight,
As shadows and beams together unite.

The universe hums in a melodic sway,
Each star has its notes, in the grand ballet.
They flicker and dance in a cosmic embrace,
Illuminating galaxies, transforming our space.

Solar flares leap like a wild, free stream,
The brilliance transcends our collective dream.
With each flicker and flash, the heavens bestow,
A timeless reminder, in the ebb and flow.

This symphony grand, it captures our soul,
In the heart of the night, we feel utterly whole.
As light shifts and sways in its intricate flight,
We hear our own voices in the shifting light.

Radiant Constellations Awaken

When twilight descends and shadows recede,
The stars emerge, lighting the world's need.
Constellations gather, a tapestry bright,
A map of our dreams in the blanket of night.

From Orion's belt to the Pleiades' glow,
Ancient tales whispered in the celestial flow.
In patterns of light, history twirls,
As the heavens unfold their secrets and swirls.

With each twinkle, a story ignites,
Of heroes and myths in the magical nights.
Galaxies spin, in an elegant dance,
As time intertwines with fate's fleeting chance.

The North Star stands tall, a beacon of hope,
Guiding wayfarers as they learn to cope.
In ethereal silence, their beauty awakens,
Radiant constellations, their promise never shaken.

Each glimmering orb, a wish on the breeze,
A flicker of longing, a moment of ease.
As slumbering eyes gaze, hearts start to dream,
In the radiant constellations, nothing's as it seems.

The Dance of Cosmic Change

In the vast expanse where the dark rivers flow,
Planets and moons put on a grand show.
Galaxies spiral in a twinkling trance,
All caught together in a cosmic dance.

Nebulas swirl, bursting with colors,
Where shadows cast light, and chaos uncovers.
In the pull of the gravity, all life will align,
The rhythm of space, a celestial design.

Each moment in time is a step in the round,
As stars whisper secrets without making a sound.
Through ages they shift, from potential to form,
In this endless ballet, universes swarm.

The darkness may linger, but light will break through,
In the folds of existence, something anew.
With twirls and with spins, the cosmos unfolds,
The dance of creation, the story retold.

In cosmic attire, we all take a stand,
Embracing the change in this vast, timeless land.
The dance of the cosmos, a song without end,
In the shimmer of stars, our hearts will ascend.

Stars in Their Evolution

In the cradle of time, they ignite bright,
Born of dust, they burst into light.
Fusing elements in a fiery embrace,
Their live cycle shows beauty and grace.

From giant to dwarf, they shift and fade,
In supernova's glow, the darkness is laid.
Whispers of hydrogen, helium's song,
In galaxies vast, they all too belong.

Life in their heart, death in their breath,
Each spark that shines, tells stories of death.
Through colors and textures, their tales unfold,
In the cosmic dance, the mysteries told.

Across the vast void, they twinkle and play,
Guiding lost souls on their astral way.
In silence they shine, eternal and bold,
A tapestry woven, a marvel to behold.

With ages unmeasured, their whispers are clear,
In the void, they shimmer, converting our fear.
Stars in their evolution, forever they'll be,
A memory etched in the night's vast sea.

When the Moon Exhales

In twilight's glow, the moon ascends,
Breathing softly as night descends.
A gentle sigh, a silver hue,
When the world closes, it starts anew.

Her beams cradle the sleeping trees,
A lullaby carried by the breeze.
Each whisper twinkles, soft and clear,
In her embrace, the night draws near.

The tides respond, they rise and fall,
In rhythm with her calming call.
The ocean hums a secret tune,
As dreams unlock beneath the moon.

When shadows stretch, and silence reigns,
Her exhale soothes, alleviates pains.
In every heart, a hopeful spark,
Guiding lost souls through the dark.

With tender light, the moon reveals,
A sanctuary where time heals.
In every glance, a story sways,
When the moon exhales, the night obeys.

The Dance of Galaxies

In the vastness, spirals twirl,
Galaxies sway, a cosmic whirl.
Graceful movement, a stellar show,
In silent rhythms, energies flow.

Through darkness deep, they intertwine,
A ballet of stars, pure and divine.
Collisions light the cosmic stage,
In their embrace, they find their rage.

Waltzing with time, they spin and glide,
In the universe, there's no divide.
Faint echoes of ancient songs,
A dance of creation where all belongs.

As nebulas burst in clouds of light,
They weave a tapestry, day into night.
And in each movement, life begins,
In the dance of galaxies, love wins.

In this ballroom where stars ignite,
We witness the beauty, pure delight.
As history swirls, dreams take flight,
In cosmic ballet, we find our sight.

Astral Alchemy

In cosmic labs, the stars combust,
Flares of gold in fine dust.
A mixture of fate, time, and space,
Alchemy of the vast embrace.

Celestial art, a crafted weave,
Galaxies formed by dreams we cleave.
Nebulae bloom in colors bold,
Their beauty whispered, a tale retold.

Each twinkle sparks a secret flame,
In this vast web, we're all the same.
Elements dance, they twist and turn,
In the heart of stars, we ever yearn.

From stardust born, our spirits rise,
In the void where darkness lies.
The universe sings an ancient hymn,
On the edge of light, our hopes swim.

The alchemist's touch, a guiding hand,
Crafts the elements across the land.
With heart and mind, it shall take flight,
In the mystery of the endless night.

Transformations of the Night Sky

A canvas deep, a shade so wide,
Stars whisper tales and dreams collide.
The dusk ignites, a glowing show,
As night unfolds, the shadows grow.

A silver veil drapes over land,
The constellations take a stand.
Wonders flicker, secrets soar,
In this realm, we all explore.

Planets dance in silent grace,
Heaven's beauty finds its place.
Veiled in mystery, dark and bright,
The sky transforms into pure light.

With cosmic winds, our hopes ascend,
To the horizon, dreams we send.
In whispered tunes, the night reveals,
The magic that the universe feels.

As dawn approaches, colors blend,
The night must yield, its reign suspend.
Yet in our hearts, the sky remains,
A constant joy, where love sustains.

The Twilight of Ascension

As day surrenders to twilight's embrace,
We rise with the stars, in this sacred space.
With whispers of light, we break through the night,
In the breath of the cosmos, we find our flight.

Moments of stillness, where dreams intertwine,
Guided by shadows, we follow the sign.
With every heartbeat, the stars will align,
In the twilight of ascension, our spirits combine.

The horizon glimmers, in hues soft and warm,
Awakening spirits, through every storm.
Amongst the still twilight, we seek our way,
In the dance of the cosmos, we shall not stray.

With wings like the constellations overhead,
We soar with the night, where passions are fed.
In twilight's embrace, fears softly dissolve,
As we rise together, our hearts resolve.

The night will not hold us, for we are the stars,
Breaking through barriers, dissolving the bars.
In the twilight of ascension, we stand hand in hand,
Together we rise, through the skies we'll expand.

Galaxies in Bloom

Petals of stardust drift through the void,
Galaxies flourish, in silence enjoyed.
Twinkling blossoms, on celestial trees,
Beauty unfurling, like whispers in breeze.

In cosmic gardens, the heavens conspire,
To bloom into light, and spiral with fire.
Colors entwine, in the universe's womb,
Creating vast wonders, where galaxies bloom.

Nebulous tendrils stretch, reaching for fate,
The canvas of night, a tapestry great.
Each star a blossom, with stories to tell,
In the heart of the cosmos, we find our swell.

Wonders are growing, forever in spin,
Galaxies twirl, as new lives begin.
The orchestra swells, in harmonious tune,
As stars rise to greet, the silvery moon.

In the expanse, where time suspends,
Galaxies bloom, as the universe bends.
Each heartbeat a ripple, in cosmic design,
A dance of creation, forever entwined.

Luminaries in Flux

Waves of starlight weave, around the night,
Planets drift softly, in oceans of light.
Constellations shimmer, in patterns unknown,
Each spark a story, in silence grown.

Fleeting auroras dance, igniting the sky,
Hearts caught in wonder, as galaxies sigh.
Time, ever shifting, a river of grace,
Luminaries flicker, in cosmic embrace.

Echoes of creation, in whispers unfold,
The universe speaks, in colors untold.
Comets rush by, with tails made of dreams,
In the fabric of night, reality gleams.

Nebula blossoms, in vibrant array,
Stars fuel the stories, that guide our way.
With each passing moment, the cosmos will shift,
As light waltzes gently, in a celestial gift.

Through the depths of the void, we seek and explore,
Luminaries in flux, forever we soar.
Finding our place, in the dance of the night,
In the heart of the cosmos, we bask in the light.

The Shifting Veils of Night

Stars whisper secrets, so soft and bright,
The moon drapes shadows, a silvery light.
Dreams dance in silence, under the sky,
While time drifts gently, a soft lullaby.

Veils of darkness shimmer, like gossamer threads,
Creatures awaken, from dreams they fled.
Fleeting moments linger, in heartbeats found,
As night embraces, a world unbound.

Clouds weave their stories, through the night air,
Veils of soft mystery, resting with care.
Whispers of nightfall, caress the trees,
Starlit confessions, carried by the breeze.

Fading light dances, on horizons wide,
Secrets of twilight, in shadows hide.
With every heartbeat, the night renews,
Painting our visions, with infinite hues.

In the stillness of night, souls find their flight,
Through shifting veils, they embrace the light.
The world is a canvas, where dreams collide,
In the magic of night, we find our guide.

Stars that Change

In the quiet of night, the stars are bright,
Each shimmering spark holds history's light.
Yet whispers of change rustle through the sky,
As constellations shift and time passes by.

Nebulae bloom in colors anew,
Transforming old tales into stories true.
Comets that wander with tails of gold,
Remind us of journeys brave and bold.

Galaxies spiral, a dance so grand,
In the rhythm of creation, we all understand.
Stars erupt in colors, a vibrant array,
Changing the canvas, night turns to day.

Every falling star brings a wish to chase,
Yet change is the constant in this infinite space.
Embrace the unknown, let your spirit soar,
For stars that change are forevermore.

In the heart of the skies, our dreams align,
Stars that shimmer, that twist, intertwine.
With every transformation, a new path will start,
Guiding us onward, igniting the heart.

The Eclipsed Evolution

In shadows of light, a dance begins,
Eclipsed moments where silence spins.
A tapestry woven of dark and bright,
Evolution thrives in the heart of night.

From ancient stardust, we rise anew,
Each eclipse a promise, a vibrant hue.
Time's gentle hand shapes what will be,
In the depths of the cosmos, we learn to see.

Celestial cycles, a rhythmic embrace,
The dance of creation, a delicate grace.
Blinded by light, yet guided by dark,
In eclipsed evolution, we find our spark.

With every occlusion, new worlds are born,
In the cradle of shadows, futures are worn.
We carve our stories in twilight's embrace,
As the stars bear witness to time and space.

So cherish the phases, the ebb and the flow,
For through the eclipses, our spirits will grow.
In the journey of change, let us find our place,
Through the eclipsed evolution, we embrace.

Celestial Reconfigurations

Stars align in patterns unknown,
Shifting sands of fate, they've grown.
Time weaves stories in shimmering space,
Celestial bodies in a waltzing race.

Galaxies collide in a cosmic embrace,
Destinies merged, lost in their trace.
Nebulae bloom, a garden of night,
Whispers of change in their radiant light.

Eclipses that filter the sun's warm face,
Dancing shadows in a timeless chase.
Planets spin tales of love and woe,
Reconfigurations in a stellar show.

In the silence of space, a soft sigh flows,
As the universe breathes, creation glows.
With each turn of orbit, a story unfolds,
Celestial secrets in starlight told.

So let us far wander where dreams take flight,
Through celestial wonders, into the night.
In the vast expanse, we'll find our way,
Amidst reconfigurations, we long to stay.

Veils of Stardust

In night's embrace, we gaze anew,
Veils of stardust dance, a shimmering view.
Whispers of dreams float in the air,
Secrets of cosmos, stories laid bare.

Galaxies twirl like lovers entwined,
Each twinkle a promise, a love redefined.
Woven in twilight, they guide our flight,
A tapestry woven with threads of light.

Upon silver shores, the heavens cast,
Reflections of futures, shadows of past.
Cradled in wonder, we chase the spark,
As echoes of stardust ignite in the dark.

The breath of the universe sighs so sweet,
With every beat, our hearts skip a beat.
Veils of stardust, a celestial stream,
In their embrace, we dare to dream.

So let us wander where the wild winds blow,
Through endless realms where the starlight flows.
Hand in hand, we'll traverse the night,
Forever entwined in the cosmic flight.

The Lunar Transition

In silver beams that softly weave,
Night embraces, we believe,
The moon whispers tales of old,
In her glow, the heart feels bold.

Cycles turning, waxing bright,
Phases painting the canvas of night,
A tranquil dance, a soothing song,
Guiding souls where they belong.

Ebbing tides of dreams and fate,
Reflecting hopes in a grand state,
Celestial rhythms, hearts align,
In these moments, stars entwine.

As shadows stretch beneath her gaze,
A tender light ignites the haze,
In moonlit paths, we find direction,
Embracing change, the lunar transition.

With every rise and gentle fall,
She calls the night, enchanting all,
Together, we dance in her light,
The lunar heart, forever bright.

Parallax of Dreams

Through the eyes of wonder we see,
Layers of time dance fluidly,
Dreams unfold in radiant streams,
Shifting views of life's grand themes.

Every heartbeat reveals a quest,
Seeking solace, a moment's rest,
In the journey, shadows ignite,
Parallax views of day and night.

Fragments of wisdom, scattered vast,
Moments cherished, shadows cast,
Chasing visions that brightly gleam,
In the essence of each dream.

Paths converge in twilight's glow,
Knowing each step, our spirits grow,
In the labyrinth, find the light,
Parallax dances, takes its flight.

As the dawn unveils its plan,
Hopes arise, united we stand,
In dreams, we find our potent might,
Parallax of promise, shining bright.

Reshaping the Universe

In the void, a spark ignites,
Colliding worlds, shifting sights,
Galaxies curve, a dance of fate,
In vast spaces, we contemplate.

Time's fabric weaves a tale so grand,
Stars align at destiny's hand,
Each moment, a ripple in the vast,
Reshaping futures, forging the past.

Nebulae blossom like dreams out wide,
Infinite wonders where secrets hide,
The cosmos sings in rhythmic grace,
In harmony, we find our place.

Echoes whisper through light-years flown,
Galactic symphonies, seeds are sown,
As we wander through stardust's flight,
Reshaping the universe, a pure delight.

Countless lives weave tales untold,
Through every challenge, brave and bold,
With every heartbeat, carve the night,
Creating stories, a future bright.

Whirlwinds of Light

In the dance of dawn's embrace,
Colors swirl in a fleeting race,
Whispers of warmth in air so bright,
Chasing shadows, igniting the night.

Nature's canvas spins and swirls,
Casting hues like pearls and curls,
Radiant beams in every sight,
Lost in the magic, pure delight.

Every moment, a spark divine,
In the chaos, a spark aligns,
Guiding hearts through gleams of flight,
Whirlwinds gathered, a mesmerizing height.

As stars twinkle in cosmic play,
Echoes of joy drift and sway,
Captured in the heart's own light,
A symphony that feels so right.

Through the currents, feelings soar,
With every pulse, we seek for more,
In this whirlwind, day turns to night,
Together, we bask in the light.

Nebulae in Bloom

In the cradle of space, nebulae bloom,
Colors exploding, dispelling the gloom.
Petals of starlight unfurling with grace,
In the heart of the cosmos, a vibrant embrace.

Swirls of creation dance in the night,
Where dreams intertwine in radiant light.
Each hue a story of worlds yet to come,
In nebulae's bloom, the universe hums.

Seeds of the future, in stardust entwined,
Radiate hope as the heavens align.
Whispers of wonder drift softly and slow,
In nebulae bloom, our spirits will grow.

Winds of the cosmos carry tales far and wide,
Dreams nurtured gently, on starlight we ride.
Awash in the colors, we rise and we swoon,
In the embrace of nebulae, we find our tune.

Galactic gardens where galaxies sigh,
Exploding with life as the stars magnify.
In the beauty of space, we weave and we loom,
United in stardust, nebulae in bloom.

Cosmic Rebirth

From ashes to stardust, a cycle divine,
Embrace of the cosmos, your spirit will shine.
Awakening softly, the universe brews,
In cosmic rebirth, we find all our hues.

Galaxies spiral in twilight's warm hold,
Echoes of laughter, the stories retold.
Veins of the cosmos pulse vibrant and clear,
In cosmic rebirth, we let go of fear.

Dust settles gently on dreams we once chased,
Filling the void of the time long replaced.
As seasons of starlight weave threads of the past,
In cosmic rebirth, our essence holds fast.

New worlds awaken beneath tender skies,
Where the whispers of ages dream and rise.
Flames of creation embrace us with grace,
In cosmic rebirth, we find our true place.

Sculpted by starlight, we dance through the night,
Each heartbeat a chapter, each moment a flight.
Through challenges faced, and choices we make,
In cosmic rebirth, our souls shall awake.

Luminous Shifts

Radiant beams of light breaking through,
Shifting the shadows, painting anew.
Each moment a canvas, colors collide,
In the depths of silence, hope will abide.

Whispers of dawn wrap the world in embrace,
Defying the darkness with delicate grace.
Time moves like water, fluid and bright,
In luminous shifts, we find our own light.

Glistening echoes of past dreams remain,
Carried on wings of the softest refrain.
From dusk into dawn, a beautiful flight,
A symphony crafted in purest delight.

Stars in the heavens like jewels that sing,
Guiding our footsteps, the joy they bring.
Embers of change flicker fervently near,
In luminous shifts, we conquer our fear.

Awakened by starlight, our journeys unfold,
An orchestra woven of stories untold.
With hearts intertwined, we wander the sea,
In luminous shifts, we are forever free.

Stardust Transitions

In the cradle of night, stars softly gleam,
Whispers of cosmos weave into a dream.
Galaxies twirl in their celestial dance,
Time stretches onward, granting a chance.

Veils of twilight embrace the unknown,
Fragments of stardust, seeds to be sown.
Each spark a story, each flicker a sigh,
Infinite journeys through the vast sky.

Twilight fades gently, a curtain drawn wide,
Hues of dusk painting the horizons' divide.
Shadows awaken, the world takes a breath,
Embracing the stillness, surrender to rest.

Stars whisper secrets in flickering glow,
Eternity beckons, inviting us slow.
In each cosmic moment, we find our own thread,
Woven in starlight, where dreams are widespread.

On celestial winds, we drift and we soar,
Navigating wonders, forever explore.
In stardust transitions, our spirits align,
A voyage of souls, through the heavens we shine.

Phoenix of the Sky

From ashes of sorrow, a flicker will rise,
Wings spread wide, painting the skies.
A flame ignited, a story reborn,
The phoenix awakens, heralding dawn.

In the heart of the fire, a fierce spirit sings,
Transcending the shadows, on golden wings.
Colors of passion painted in flight,
Illuminate dreams through the depths of night.

With each new horizon, hope takes its form,
Soaring above, through the calm and the storm.
Ancient the journey, yet vibrant with grace,
In the phoenix's path, we find our own place.

The cycle of life written bold in the sky,
When one fades away, another will fly.
Through the skies bright and endless we glide,
Embracing all moments with the phoenix as guide.

With wings of resilience, our hearts burn anew,
From the ashes of yesterday, we rise and pursue.
In the flames of existence, we learn to be free,
The phoenix of the sky is the spirit of me.

Vortex of the Cosmos

Swirling colors in endless delight,
A vortex of wonders, twirling through night.
Stars collide softly, creating new dreams,
In cosmic ballet, a dance of extremes.

Galaxies spiral, each moment a thrill,
Echoes of ages, the universe still.
Gravity pulling, a tender embrace,
In the vortex of cosmos, we find our place.

Through tunnels of starlight, we drift and we fly,
Chasing the whispers of galaxies high.
Lost in the magic, we willingly roam,
Within the endless, we always find home.

In shadows of giants, we twinkle and glow,
All our connections, an intricate flow.
Time blurs like stardust, in spirals we seek,
Vortex of the cosmos, vibrant and unique.

As dimensions entwine, our fates intertwist,
In this cosmic waltz, no dreams are dismissed.
Embraced by the vastness, we dance in delight,
In the heart of the vortex, we welcome the night.

The Birth of Starlight

In the cradle of time, night meets its dawn,
Whispers of cosmic birth, softly drawn.
Fingers of light stretch across the domain,
Awakening dreams in a graceful refrain.

A spark ignites in the vastness of space,
Swirling clouds gather, begin to embrace.
Colors explode in a beautiful dance,
The birth of starlight, a stellar romance.

Nebulas cradle the nascent flame,
Writing the stories that none can claim.
In this wild chaos, beauty takes flight,
Witness, the wonder, the birth of starlight.

Galactic whispers intertwine and blend,
Light years apart, yet, let love transcend.
The universe hums with radiant delight,
As distant hearts marvel at starlight.

With every twinkle, a story unfolds,
Old as the cosmos, yet brand new and bold.
In the silence of night, we come to ignite,
Our spirits unite at the birth of starlight.

Nebulous Nurturing

In twilight's embrace, dreams softly grow,
Veils of the night, a gentle flow.
Stars whisper secrets in silvery hues,
Cradled in shadows, a world to choose.

Misty tendrils weave through the air,
Gentle caresses, a cosmic prayer.
Colors awaken, in dances so light,
Nurtured by silence, deep in the night.

Crystals of stardust on soft velvet skies,
Illuminate wishes, bright like our sighs.
In the heart of darkness, a promise takes flight,
Nebulous nurturing, a heartwarming sight.

Galaxies spin in a graceful embrace,
Time drips slowly, a standard pace.
Beneath this vastness, we cherish our fate,
In nebulous gardens, we patiently wait.

A lullaby whispers through twilight's retreat,
With every heartbeat, our souls softly meet.
Bound by the cosmos, we grow and we thrive,
In nebulous warmth, we feel so alive.

The Metamorphosis of Infinity

In the cradle of time, we begin,
A spark ignites, the dance within.
From dust of stars, we rise and spin,
The metamorphosis of infinity's grin.

Eons pass, yet we remain bound,
Through cycles endless, where dreams are found.
In every heartbeat, a cosmic sound,
In the tapestry, we are crowned.

Transformations weave in every breath,
Life and death, a sacred depth.
In the whispers of the cosmos, we heft,
A metamorphosis, from love, we're kept.

Through shadow and light, we learn to see,
Infinity's mirror reflects our glee.
In every moment, a chance to be,
The metamorphosis of you and me.

In the end, we flow like the sea,
Into the cosmos, eternally free.
Through time and space, our spirits agree,
A journey unending, a grand decree.

Celestial Journeys

Through the starlit skies we roam,
On celestial journeys, far from home.
Galactic highways, we freely comb,
In the universe, we find our tome.

Planets whisper, they call our name,
In this vast expanse, nothing's the same.
With shooting stars, we stake our claim,
Every moment, a flickering flame.

Comets race with tails of light,
In cosmic ballet, they take flight.
We navigate through day and night,
Guided by dreams, hope in sight.

In constellations, stories reside,
Lost in wonder, we cannot hide.
Among the stars, our spirits glide,
On celestial journeys, side by side.

We learn the truths that stardust shares,
In timeless dance, no need for cares.
With every journey, love ensnares,
Cosmic travelers, unbound, we dare.

From Void to Vibration

From the void, a whisper grows,
Vibrations dance where silence flows.
Frequencies blend, as energy knows,
The pulse of life, the cosmos shows.

Einstein's dreams, a leap through space,
Relativity in this sacred place.
Moments tangle, time's embrace,
From void to vibration, we trace.

Echoes ripple through the night,
As souls connect, hearts take flight.
In harmony, we find our light,
A cosmic bond, a shared delight.

Resonating in the depths within,
Each heartbeat sings, where dreams begin.
In this dance, there is no sin,
From void to vibration, we spin.

In the end, we return anew,
From void to vibration, it's true.
In every star, in every hue,
A cosmic journey, me and you.

Cosmic Infusion

Stars whisper secrets in the night,
Galaxies dance, a cosmic sight.
Waves of energy, pure and bright,
Time and space in endless flight.

Nebulas bloom, colors collide,
Celestial rivers, a cosmic tide.
Mysteries swirl, nowhere to hide,
In the vastness, we confide.

Light years drift in silence deep,
In cosmic dreams, we softly sleep.
Awake we are, memories to keep,
In the universe, a bond we reap.

Planets spin with tales to tell,
In orbits wide, under their spell.
The fabric of time, a resonant bell,
Cosmic infusion, we dwell.

In the end, we all return,
To stardust, where we will burn.
A cycle endless, we discern,
From cosmic ashes, hope we earn.

Celestial Echoes

In the night, a whisper calls,
Echoing through celestial halls.
Stars align, their voices clear,
Murmurs of the universe near.

Through the void, we hear the song,
A harmony that feels so strong.
Each note, a story shared in grace,
In the cosmos, we find our place.

From distant realms, the echoes flow,
Carrying secrets we yearn to know.
Chasing comets as they glide,
Following dreams that swell inside.

In the stillness, they impart,
Wisdom echoing in the heart.
Celestial tides that pull and sway,
Guiding us along the way.

In the symphony of night,
We find solace, pure delight.
Every echo brings us near,
To what we seek, the path is clear.

From Chaos to Harmony

In the tempest, voices rise,
Clashing waves and angry skies.
Yet within the storm's embrace,
Lies a hope for gentle grace.

Threads of discord weave the night,
Yearning for the dawn's soft light.
In the silence, truths unwind,
Beauty etched in every mind.

With every clash, a lesson learned,
From embers, brighter futures burned.
Chaos whispers of the past,
Striving towards the peace to last.

Harmony begins to bloom,
Filling up the darkest room.
With each note of unity,
A brighter world, we come to see.

Through storms, we find the way,
Guided by the light of day.
From chaos, strength we glean,
In harmony, we begin to dream.

Aurora's Metamorphosis

Dancing lights in morning's veil,
Whispers of a radiant tale.
Colors swirl in soft embrace,
Nature's brush, a cosmic grace.

Softly, she begins to rise,
Painting warmth across the skies.
From night's grasp, she breaks away,
Bringing forth the break of day.

Crimson flecks and golden hues,
In her glow, the world renews.
Every dawn, a new rebirth,
Lighting up our storied earth.

With each stroke, the shadows flee,
Opening the heart to see.
A promise bright in every ray,
Hopes fulfilled, come what may.

In the quiet, magic grows,
Through the light, our spirit flows.
Aurora calls us to the light,
In her dance, our souls take flight.

The Ascension of Stars

In the silent sky they rise,
Twinkling gems, the night's surprise.
Whispers of light in the dark,
Each one tells a tale, a spark.

Through the velvet depths, they soar,
Guiding wishes from the shore.
A tapestry of dreams unfurl,
In the vastness, hearts can twirl.

They spark the moon to dance with pride,
As shadows stretch and softly glide.
In their glow, we find our way,
Every night, a brand new play.

Celestial light, a gentle guide,
Holding secrets, deep inside.
As we gaze, our troubles fade,
In their presence, hopes are laid.

With every blink, they shine anew,
Painting skies in shades of blue.
We are all beneath their gaze,
Lost in wonder, we remain.

Transitions of Time and Space

Moments slip like grains of sand,
Each second shifts a steady hand.
In every heartbeat, life's command,
Transitions sweep across the land.

Seasons turn in fluid grace,
Painting beauty on nature's face.
In every change, we find our place,
Embracing time as we embrace.

Time dances softly, never still,
Carving futures with an iron will.
Every breath, a chance to fulfill,
In the tapestry, dreams instill.

From dawn to dusk, the world reshapes,
Crafting tales as the sun escapes.
In shifting shadows, fate drapes,
Life unfolds in countless tapes.

The cosmos breathes in whispers low,
A rhythm where unknowns will flow.
Through transitions, we learn to grow,
In time and space, our hearts will glow.

Stellar Migrations

Constellations swirl in cosmic dance,
Drifting freely, guided by chance.
Galaxies whisper, stirring romance,
In the vast expanse, we take a glance.

Stars travel paths through time and space,
Borne on winds in a timeless race.
From ancient shores to new embrace,
Each twinkle holds a storied trace.

Planets spin in a silken thread,
Echoes of light where dreams are bred.
In the night sky, pathways spread,
A map of wishes, carefully led.

Celestial bodies, silent guides,
Navigating through the cosmic tides.
In their journeys, hope resides,
As we watch, our heart abides.

The universe calls in a soft hush,
Inviting souls to feel the rush.
In stellar migrations, dreams don't crush,
But flourish bright in cosmic blush.

Fluctuating Horizons

The sun plays hide and seek with skies,
Where golden hues in silence rise.
Clouds drift lazily, sweet surprise,
As daylight dips and softly sighs.

Mountains stand guard, their shadows grow,
Embracing valleys, where rivers flow.
Each moment changes, fast or slow,
In the dance of light, we feel the glow.

Horizons blend with colors bright,
A tapestry of day and night.
In every glance, a new delight,
With shifting shades, the world takes flight.

Winds carry whispers from afar,
Tales of hope beneath each star.
The horizon beckons, never mar,
Inviting dreams where journeys are.

As starlight hints of paths unsaid,
The future waits, alive, widespread.
In every heartbeat, thoughts are bred,
Fluctuating hopes, the spirit fed.

The Changing Face of Night

The stars begin to glow bright,
As shadows dance in fading light.
The moon hangs low, a silver sight,
Embracing all with gentle might.

Whispers of dreams on a cool breeze,
Rustling leaves tell tales with ease.
The night unfolds, a canvas tease,
Inviting hearts to find their peace.

A lullaby from distant shores,
Crickets sing, the night implores.
In twilight's charm, the spirit soars,
While silence weaves through open doors.

Stars blink like secrets in the dark,
Flickering souls, a cosmic spark.
In hush, the universe leaves a mark,
Guiding the lost to find their arc.

With each hour, the colors shift,
Creating moods, a wondrous gift.
Through veils of dreams, we drift and lift,
Until the dawn, the night will sift.

Radiance in Flux

In the twilight where shadows play,
Radiance erupts in hues of gray.
Fluctuating light paints the air,
A tapestry woven, vibrant and rare.

Stars blink softly in the vast night,
Unveiling paths with celestial light.
The universe whispers of change so bright,
Radiance flowing, kaleidoscopic sight.

As comets dance, tracing silent trails,
In the shimmering silence, magic prevails.
Each flicker carries a memory's spark,
Illuminating dreams drifting in the dark.

Meteors blaze, symbols of fate,
In the flux of time, we hesitate.
Yet in their glow, a truth does lie,
Radiance in flux, it will never die.

Embrace the journey through cosmic seas,
With every pulse, we draw in the breeze.
In the heart of chaos, beauty sings,
Radiance in flux, the light it brings.

The Changes of Celestia

In the garden of stars, where whispers roam,
Celestia shifts, it carves a home.
Light and shadow play their game,
Each fleeting moment never the same.

Bubbles of brightness burst in the void,
As colors blend, once destroyed.
Winds of change sweep across the plains,
Chasing echoes of forgotten names.

Every dawn invites a new start,
As echoes of dusk pull at the heart.
Celestia dances with a graceful air,
In her embrace, we lose despair.

The beauty lies in the complex hue,
Transformations from old to new.
Galaxies swirl in a radiant glow,
In the fabric of time, the changes flow.

With each heartbeat, worlds collide,
In celestial wonders, there's nowhere to hide.
Embrace the changes, let go of the past,
In the sky's embrace, we find peace at last.

Tides of the Universe

Waves of stardust crash on shores unseen,
Flowing softly, like a gentle dream.
Gravity pulls on the heart of the sea,
While the cosmos breathes in harmony.

Moonlight dips in a silver tide,
The ocean's depths, where secrets hide.
Galactic currents pull and sway,
Guiding the souls that dare to stray.

Celestial bodies mark the way,
As the tides awaken at break of day.
Stars write stories on celestial sand,
Drawing close, yet forever unplanned.

Planets revolve in a cosmic dance,
In the ebb and flow, we find our chance.
Waves of time wash over past and future,
An endless cycle, a timeless suture.

With each tide, a new path appears,
In the vast universe, we shed our fears.
For in the rhythm of the celestial sea,
We find our place, where we're meant to be.

Celestial Shapeshifting

In the quiet of the night, a star bends,
Shapes are shifting, as the light descends.
A cosmic dance unfolds, in endless skies,
Where time is fluid, and fate complies.

Reflections glimmer on the moon's face,
Whispers of dreams in a timeless space.
Galaxies collide, a radiant swirl,
In the silence, secrets unfurl.

Nebulas weave tales of forgotten lore,
Constellations shifting, forevermore.
Reshape the darkness with a touch so light,
Embrace the shadows, embrace the night.

Across the void, energies embrace,
A tapestry woven, in cosmic grace.
From dusk till dawn, the universe plays,
In every moment, the rhythm sways.

Stars transform in the twilight's hue,
Colors melting into shades anew.
Celestial bodies, in constant flight,
Forever changing, like day to night.

Ether's Metamorphosis

In silence deep, the ether breathes,
A canvas vast, where spirit weaves.
With fleeting thoughts and whispered dreams,
In every heart, a spark redeems.

Transforming thoughts like flowing streams,
Ethereal dance, the world redeems.
In shadows cast, foundations shift,
Life's intricate, luminous gift.

Through realms unseen, the currents run,
In every tear, a story spun.
A tapestry of colors blend,
In every fragment, love transcends.

From matter's touch to radiant glow,
An endless cycle, seeds to sow.
With every breath, existence hums,
Evolving forms in laughter's drums.

The cosmic dance, a sacred sway,
In every night, and every day.
With each shift, the world aligns,
In ether's arms, the heart refines.

The Evolving Sky

Morning breaks with tender grace,
A canvas wide, the clouds embrace.
Colors clash, and shadows play,
As dreams unfold with light of day.

From azure peaks to storms so bold,
The tales of time and space unfold.
A tapestry of whispers high,
In every glance, the shifting sky.

Evening falls with hues of gold,
The whispers of the night unfold.
Stars awaken, stories breathe,
In every twinkle, hope weaves.

Each change a tale of ages past,
In every cloud, a shadow cast.
The moonlight spills, ethereal thread,
In nightly dreams, our fears are shed.

Through storms and calm, the sky expands,
A realm of wonders, wild and grand.
In every glance, a world anew,
The evolving sky, our hearts pursue.

From Nova to Neutron

A stellar birth, a radiant show,
In cosmic storms, the fiery glow.
Exploding hearts, they pierce the night,
Transforming chaos into light.

Fragments scatter, across the space,
In swirling dance, they find their place.
From fiery depths to tranquil hum,
A neutron star, the silence comes.

Gravity's grip holds tightly fast,
A fusion heart, the die is cast.
In iron cores, the secrets churn,
From ancient winds, new fires burn.

Each pulse a whisper, strong yet meek,
Vibrations echo, tales they speak.
The universe, a symphony,
Of ancient light, eternity.

Mark the skies where dark once reigned,
From ashes born, the stars regained.
The journey brief, but brilliance vast,
In every death, a life amassed.

Light's Transformation

In the dawn, a whisper glows,
Casting shadows, softly flows.
Colors dance, and warmth ignites,
As day unfolds its golden sights.

Through prisms bright, the hues appear,
Each spectrum sings, the world so clear.
With every shift, our visions bloom,
In nature's light, we find our room.

Moments shift from dusk to dawn,
In twilight's grip, the magic's drawn.
As stars emerge, the night ignites,
The cosmos weaves its endless sights.

Invisible waves in the air,
Traveling far with silent care.
Bending time, they weave and sway,
In every heartbeat, light's ballet.

From bright to faint, each pulse remains,
In every flicker, love sustains.
The journey of the bright and dark,
Illuminates the hidden spark.

When Comets Rewrite Their Tales

Across the sky, a comet trails bright,
With longing, it arcs through the velvet night.
A fleeting moment, destiny's call,
Changing the paths of one and all.

In whispers of starlight, old stories unwind,
Legends forgotten in the cosmic mind.
As comets race, history bends,
Rewriting the tales that time cannot end.

With each blazing heart, our spirits unite,
Chasing the echoes that dance in the light.
Past and future entwining tight,
In the glow of a comet, we find our flight.

As fragments of time scatter like seeds,
New stories sprout from the timeless needs.
When comets soar, magic unfolds,
Transforming the myths that the universe holds.

So let us embrace the celestial path,
Finding our truths in the comet's wrath.
With every return, a chance to begin,
In the vastness above, our journeys spin.

Nebulae's Embrace

In cosmic gardens of swirling hues,
Where stardust births old and new views.
Nebulae cradle stars in their sway,
Whispering secrets of night and day.

Colors collide in a brilliant song,
Celestial bodies dance all night long.
Patterns emerge in the vibrant glow,
A tapestry woven where spirits flow.

In this embrace, we find our place,
A union of time, space, and grace.
Each twinkle a promise, a tale yet told,
In the arms of the universe, brave and bold.

Moments stretch in a cosmic treat,
Life's dance unfolding, bittersweet.
Through the turning of worlds, we dare to dream,
In the heart of nebulae, we forever beam.

As light fades gently into the blue,
Nebulae hold a world fresh and true.
In their soft embrace, we wander free,
Eternal guardians of our destiny.

Moonlight's Whisper of Transformation

Beneath the gaze of a silvered moon,
Night's soft lullaby hums a tune.
Shadows flicker, breathing anew,
In this magic, all things accrue.

The forest sighs, cloaked in grace,
Pathways beckon with a secret face.
Leaves rustle softly, wisdom shared,
Embracing the truth that all are dared.

Reflections shimmer on still waters,
A dance of fate, as time whispers.
In the quiet, spirits take flight,
Guided by dreams in the soft moonlight.

Transformation woven in silken threads,
Where fear dissolves and courage spreads.
With every heartbeat, a world reborn,
As souls awaken to the dawn's warm scorn.

In moonlit silence, we find our way,
Transforming shadows into bright day.
Embrace the whispers that call your name,
In every heartbeat, we stoke the flame.

The Alchemy of Astral Dreams

In twilight shimmers, shadows dance,
Starlit visions, secret romance.
Celestial realms weave threads of gold,
Awakening dreams, soft yet bold.

Whispers of cosmos drift through the night,
Each sigh a spark, igniting the light.
Mystic colors spill from the sky,
Painting the silence, where echoes lie.

Galaxies swirl in a velvet embrace,
Time and space shift in a silken chase.
Through the dark, we find our way,
Guided by stardust, we long to stay.

Fragmented hopes on the edges gleam,
Crafted by hands of a wandering dream.
In this alchemy, hearts intertwine,
Creating a tapestry, delicate and fine.

As dawn approaches, the dreams must fade,
Leaving behind a universe made.
Yet in our hearts, those moments gleam,
Forever etched in the fabric of dream.

Celestial Sorcery

In the stillness, magic brews,
Cosmic forces, guiding clues.
Celestial spells in the air,
Woven softly, everywhere.

Stardust drips from heaven's hand,
Painting visions across the land.
Planets spin their ancient song,
In this vastness, we belong.

Shooting stars ignite the sky,
A moment's wish, a fleeting fly.
Galaxies swirl, a cosmic night,
Twinkling softly, pure delight.

In this realm where shadows play,
Wonders bloom and drift away.
Each heartbeat, a pulse of fate,
In this dance, we integrate.

With the dawn, the magic stays,
Echoing in subtle ways.
In our hearts, the cosmos flows,
Celestial sorcery bestows.

The Veil of Night

A curtain drapes, the day departs,
Enveloping the world in arts.
Stars peer through the velvet screen,
In shadows, secrets often glean.

Moonbeams spill on silver streams,
Underneath, a world of dreams.
Night's embrace, a soft caress,
In the dark, we find our rest.

Gentle breezes whisper low,
Carrying tales from long ago.
Through the quiet, echoes play,
Guiding hearts till break of day.

Each flicker holds a universe,
Silent prayer, a soft converse.
In the stillness, thoughts take flight,
Wrapped in the veil of night.

Every shadow, every spark,
Hiding stories, bright and stark.
As the stars begin to gleam,
We awaken to the dream.

Stellar Reawakening

From the ashes of the dawn,
Stars ignite, the night is drawn.
In the silence of the void,
Cosmic wonders, not destroyed.

Galaxies in swirling dance,
In the dark, they take their chance.
Nebulae with colors bright,
Breathing life into the night.

Whispers of the ancient past,
Secrets hidden, shadows cast.
Celestial bodies sway and spin,
Tales of worlds that were, begin.

Time unfolds like rippling streams,
Interstellar, weaving dreams.
Events unravel, pure delight,
As we gaze into the night.

With each blink, the stars align,
Patterns form, a grand design.
In the cosmos, vast and wide,
Wonder waits on every side.

Twilight Transfigurations

In the hush of dusk's embrace,
Colors blend in soft embrace.
Whispers of the coming night,
Stars emerge, a twinkling sight.

Shadows stretch along the ground,
Nature's peace is all around.
Crickets sing their evening song,
As the world hums along.

Clouds turn pink, then fade to gray,
Birds return to nest and stay.
Each breath deep, a sigh of calm,
Twilight's glow, an evening balm.

Glimmers dance on water's face,
Life slows down, a gentle pace.
Fading light, the day's goodbye,
Underneath the vast, dark sky.

Nighttime's curtain softly falls,
Moonlight whispers, softly calls.
Stars awaken, one by one,
In the quiet, day is done.

Whispers of Cosmic Transition

In silence, the cosmos breathes and sighs,
Stars flicker on as the old one dies.
Galaxies merge in a cosmic embrace,
In the void, a magical space.

The light of dawn breaks shadows anew,
In every shift, the old meets the true.
A symphony rising in colors profound,
As whispers of change are woven around.

Time holds the echoes of what once was,
The universe bends in a poetic pause.
In stellar winds, our dreams take flight,
Guided by the soft glow of night.

With every heartbeat, the cosmos sways,
Embracing the beauty of time's ballet.
In the dance of existence, we find our place,
A whisper of hope in the vastness of space.

The Transformation of Time

Moments shift like sands of gold,
Tales of the ages, quietly told.
From dawn to dusk, the shadows grow,
An endless cycle, a ceaseless flow.

Seasons change in whispered breath,
Life, a tapestry woven with death.
In every heartbeat, the past resides,
In each new dawn, the future hides.

Time is a river, ever vast,
Carving pathways from the past.
In its embrace, we learn to bend,
As we weave and mend, and find our end.

The seconds dance, a fleeting tease,
Moments gathered like autumn leaves.
In every tick, a story spun,
A journey shared, we become one.

Planets in Resonance

In the dark abyss, they spin and glide,
Planets of wonder, side by side.
A symphony played on cosmic strings,
In harmony, the universe sings.

Distant worlds with secrets to share,
Echoes of life linger in the air.
Galaxies twirl in an endless dance,
Each planet holds a cosmic chance.

With every rotation, time is reborn,
The fabric of space, both worn and torn.
Fates intertwined in a ballet so grand,
Connected we are, hand in hand.

Across the void, their whispers flow,
Stories of ages, we yearn to know.
In starlit nights, we dream and pine,
For the touch of the world divine.

Aurora's Changing Gaze

In twilight's gentle breath, we sigh,
The colors dance as night draws nigh.
Auroras flicker, bold and bright,
A canvas painted, pure delight.

Under the heavens, shadows play,
With whispers of hope at the end of day.
The north winds carry a tale so grand,
Of dreams unfurling in this vast land.

Stars in the distance twinkle softly,
Lighting the path we walk so softly.
A tapestry woven, time slips by,
In awe, we gather, hearts lifted high.

Embrace the moment, let it flow,
Feel the pulse of the earth below.
In every hue, a story lies,
In Aurora's gaze, our spirit flies.

Starborn Transitions

In the cradle of the void,
Stars awaken from dreams,
With each breath, joy deployed,
Creating new light beams.

Merging destinies flow,
Across galaxies wide,
In the dance of the glow,
Weaving worlds side by side.

Emerald hues arise,
From stardust, we transform,
In the endless skies,
Where creation is born.

Each flicker tells a tale,
Of the journeys we take,
With the cosmos to sail,
In the ripples we make.

Starborn souls shall ignite,
In the tapestry spun,
Through darkness and light,
We are many, yet one.

Fading into Eternity

As dusk meets the dawn's glow,
Releasing the time we hold,
In whispers, we come and go,
Stories of life unfold.

With each breath, we transcend,
Like shadows in the sun,
In moments that never end,
Our journey's just begun.

Silent echoes remain,
In the void of the night,
Colors blur, free from pain,
Drifting into the light.

Time weaves a gentle thread,
A tapestry of dreams,
In the words left unsaid,
Life's fleeting, tender themes.

As we fade, we ignite,
In the shimmer of stars,
Caught in this cosmic flight,
No boundaries, no bars.

Quantum Drift

Fleeting thoughts intertwine,
In the vast cosmic weave,
Moments bend and realign,
What we grasp, we believe.

Through dimensions we soar,
Past the veil of our mind,
Seeking what lies in store,
In the fabric we find.

Particles whisper and spin,
In the dance of the light,
Lost where the worlds begin,
In the stillness of night.

Echoes of time collide,
In a spiral embrace,
Each heartbeat, a guide,
In the ever-changing space.

In quantum's gentle sway,
We drift through the unknown,
Finding paths that will play,
In the seeds we have sown.

Ethereal Dance

In twilight's gentle embrace,
Whispers of shadows play,
The moonlight weaves a lace,
In the night's soft ballet.

Twinkling stars in the sky,
Echoes of dreams take flight,
Beneath a watchful eye,
The world's lost in the light.

Soft winds carry a song,
Of voices long gone by,
In this realm, we belong,
Where silence meets the sky.

Every heartbeat aligned,
With the rhythm of grace,
In the stillness, we find,
A timeless, sacred space.

Together we shall sway,
In a dance so divine,
As night gives way to day,
In a moment, we shine.

Illuminated Existences

In the morning light, we rise,
Painting dreams across the skies.
Every heartbeat sings a song,
Illuminated, we belong.

Colors blend in vibrant hues,
Each moment sharing all our views.
With hands entwined, we create,
A tapestry of love and fate.

In this life where spirits dance,
We embrace each fleeting chance.
Laughter echoes, fills the air,
Illuminated by our care.

Through trials faced and joys we've known,
We find the strength within us grown.
Together shining, bold and bright,
Illuminated in the night.

Existences, intertwining fast,
In the light, our shadows cast.
United in a single breath,
In love's embrace, we conquer death.

Shadows of the Cosmos

In the hush of night, stars gleam,
Casting shadows on a dream.
Whispers ride on cosmic winds,
Where the silence softly spins.

Nebulas in hues so bright,
Cradle secrets of the night.
Galactic tales in tones obscure,
In shadows, ancient truths endure.

Floating in this ocean vast,
We glimpse the future, weave the past.
Each twinkling light, a story told,
In the blackness, mysteries unfold.

Echoes of the worlds unseen,
Shape our thoughts, our hopes between.
Fractals dance in space's breath,
Life and beauty weave through death.

Shadows play in cosmic chase,
Each movement a divine embrace.
In the stillness, we reside,
Finding home where shadows bide.

Universe in Flux

Galaxies spin in the dark,
With each twist, they leave a mark.
Time slips through like grains of sand,
In the cosmos, vast and grand.

Planets drift, their paths unknown,
In a dance of fate they've grown.
Stars collide and give us birth,
Creating wonders, rich in worth.

Amidst the chaos, beauty reigns,
In every heartbeat, joy remains.
As constellations shift and sway,
We find our dreams, they light the way.

Eternal cycles, rise and fall,
Whispers echo, nature's call.
In this universe, ever wide,
We navigate the cosmic tide.

The fabric weaves what's lost and found,
In the silence, wisdom's sound.
As we journey through the flux,
Our spirits soar, love's gentle nux.

Lunar Embers

In the night sky, embers glow,
Casting light on dreams below.
Whispers of the stars align,
In the quiet, worlds entwine.

Moonlit beams on silver streams,
Carrying the weight of dreams.
Softly wrapped in twilight's grace,
Time slows down in this embrace.

Night unfolds its velvet cloak,
While fires in the shadows stoke.
Echoes dance on breezes light,
As the universe ignites.

Celestial stories softly flow,
From the hearts of those who know.
With each flicker, hope ignites,
Guided by the lunar lights.

In this realm where spirits soar,
We find the magic, evermore.
Lunar embers, gentle sighs,
Holding secrets of the skies.

Skies in Flux: A Celestial Tale

The heavens shift, a dance so grand,
Where clouds and stars together stand.
In hues of orange, pink, and blue,
A story written for me and you.

As daylight wanes, the twilight sings,
Unveiling all that starlight brings.
A canvas stretched, forever wise,
Painted softly by tender skies.

Constellations weave the night,
In ancient tales of love and fight.
Each twinkle a word in a cosmic song,
Reminding us of where we belong.

The moon, a guardian of silent dreams,
Glows brightly in silvered beams.
And as the universe breathes with pride,
The essence of wonder we cannot hide.

So we watch the skies in endless awe,
Beneath a blanket, the world we draw.
For in the flux of starry night,
Lies the magic of endless flight.

Chasing Wormholes

Through the vastness, we do roam,
Seeking paths that lead us home.
Wormholes swirl, a beckoning sight,
Through time and space, we take our flight.

With every leap, dimensions shift,
A cosmic dance, the universe's gift.
We chase the unknown, bold and brave,
In the depths, where mysteries wave.

Stars whisper secrets from afar,
Guiding travelers, every star.
In the spiral, dreams collide,
Where courage and wonder coincide.

With each venture, reality distorts,
Into realms where adventure cavorts.
In that instant, we slip and glide,
Through the fabric of time, we reside.

So let us chase those cosmic trails,
Beyond horizons where hope prevails.
In the embrace of the great unknown,
Together we venture, never alone.

The Metamorphosis of Light

When dawn breaks, shadows flee,
Colors bloom, wild and free.
Sunrise paints the world anew,
Touching hearts with golden hue.

As night surrenders to the day,
Light casts darkness far away.
In every ray, a story told,
Of whispers soft and visions bold.

The dance of dusk and dawn unfolds,
Painting skies in fiery golds.
Day and night in gentle embrace,
In this rhythm, we find our place.

Through prisms bright, the colors bend,
Transforming light, like time, won't end.
Each glimmer holds a spark divine,
In every shade, the stars align.

So let us chase the fleeting glow,
As light reveals what hearts bestow.
In the metamorphosis, we learn,
That every heartbeat shall return.

Beyond the Horizon of Stars

In the stillness of the night,
Dreams take flight like kites.
Beyond the reach of moon's glow,
What wonders lie, we do not know.

Galaxies spin in silent dance,
Fueling hope in every glance.
Countless worlds await our sight,
Beneath the endless cosmic light.

Whispers of comets trace the sky,
While distant echoes softly sigh.
Twinkling gems in a velvet sea,
Guiding hearts to what could be.

Each sparkle holds a mystery deep,
A promise that the stars will keep.
In their glow, our spirits rise,
Searching for truths beyond the skies.

So we gaze at twilight's end,
With wishes laced, our dreams extend.
For in the cosmos, vast and wide,
Lies the magic we abide.

Shadows of the Infinite Realm

In shadows deep where echoes dwell,
The infinite sings its secret spell.
Mysteries wrapped in twilight's guise,
In the darkness, wisdom lies.

Unseen paths weave through the night,
Guiding souls by gentle light.
Each shadow holds a tale of old,
In whispers soft, their truths unfold.

The realm expands, yet time stands still,
Each heartbeat echoes, strong, and will.
In quietude, the cosmos breathes,
In shadows, life weaves and seethes.

From dusk till dawn, we roam and weave,
A tapestry of dreams, we grieve.
In shadows deep, our souls find peace,
In the infinite realm, we cease.

The Rebirth of Celestial Bodies

From ashes born, the stars revive,
Cosmic dance where dreams arrive.
In the birth of light anew,
Celestial bodies find their hue.

Nebulas bloom in vibrant shades,
In the cosmos, beauty trades.
Galaxies spin, a graceful twirl,
In their rebirth, worlds unfurl.

Time unwinds, the old gives way,
Stars emerge to greet the day.
Darkness yields to radiant fire,
Celestial dreams take us higher.

Fusions spark in twilight's breath,
In the cradle of life and death.
From stardust, new horizons rise,
In cosmic whispers, hear the sighs.

Echoes of Eclipsed Souls

In shadows cast by ancient light,
Souls eclipse both day and night.
Whispers linger, dark and deep,
In their silence, secrets keep.

Time stands still, a patient ghost,
In longing, echoes rise the most.
Fading shadows chase the sun,
In their silence, we are one.

Memories like flickering stars,
Reveal the wounds, the silent scars.
Lost in twilight's gentle hold,
Stories etched in silence told.

Through the void, a haunting call,
Each soul echoes, rise or fall.
In the dusk, we find our way,
In silence, night bleeds into day.

From Stardust to Silence

In the void where whispers play,
Stardust glimmers, fades away.
Echoes linger, soft and light,
Carried by the hush of night.

Galaxies weave their ancient tale,
In the stillness, dreams set sail.
Time's embrace, a tender fold,
In silence, stories left untold.

Fragments lost in cosmic seas,
Gravity holds, yet we are free.
Stars ignite, then dimly sigh,
In the silence, we learn to fly.

A journey forged in endless space,
Moments fleeting, leaving trace.
From stardust to eternal peace,
In silence, our souls find release.

Nova's Awakening

In the void where silence dwells,
A whisper sparks, a story tells.
From darkened ashes, flames arise,
Giving birth to luminous skies.

Stars erupt in a brilliant show,
Colors burst, a radiant flow.
In cosmic tumult, a heartbeat roars,
Nova awakens, forever soars.

Twilight shimmers, shadows dissolve,
Mysteries of light, we evolve.
Each explosion a life anew,
In the dance of time, infinity's view.

Across the canvas, galaxies spin,
In wondrous arcs where dreams begin.
The universe hums a gentle tune,
As novas light the path to noon.

With every flare, a message clear,
In the chaos, beauty appears.
A cycle eternal, in time we blend,
Innova's grace, love without end.

The Sky's Renaissance

Awake! The dawn heralds the day,
A vibrant canvas begins to play.
Pastels meet in morning's kiss,
Each hue a promise, a gentle bliss.

Clouds, like brushes, paint the blue,
Strokes of white, softened and true.
In the theater of expansive skies,
Nature's wonders awaken our sighs.

As sunlight spills, the shadows flee,
Illuminating all there can be.
A renaissance reborn, anew,
In every breath, the world feels true.

Birds take wing, dancing in air,
Echoes of freedom, beyond compare.
Voices rise in harmonious song,
Reminding us where we belong.

With twilight's blush, the colors blend,
A masterpiece that will never end.
In the sky's embrace, we find our chance,
To revel in life's eternal dance.

Dreamweaver of the Cosmos

In the cradle of starlight's gleam,
A weaver spins a silver dream.
Galaxies shimmer in cosmic flow,
Where wishes wander, and hopes grow.

Through the fabric of endless night,
Colors twine in radiant flight.
Every thought a thread of fate,
Crafting futures we contemplate.

Eclipsed in whispers, worlds collide,
Dreams unfurl like a cosmic tide.
Awakened by the silent call,
The weaver beckons, embracing all.

From nebulae to space's core,
Every heartbeat opens a door.
In the tapestry, stories blend,
A luminous journey that has no end.

With each stitch, a new tale spun,
Unraveled threads, together run.
In the heart of stars, truth is found,
As dreamweavers paint the vast profound.

Ethereal Transformations

Whispers of change dance in the night,
Softly they mold shadows into light.
In the silence where spirits roam,
Each heartbeat knows it's found a home.

Waves of essence ebb and flow,
Carrying secrets we long to know.
In the stillness, a spark ignites,
Transforming dreams into new heights.

Glimmers twirl in twilight's embrace,
Nature reflects a sacred space.
Colors shift, a vibrant scene,
Revealing what has always been.

In the heart of the unseen world,
Mysteries in vision unfurled.
Life's canvas, painted from within,
Emerging cycles, rebirth begins.

With each breath, the cosmos sighs,
In unity where the spirit flies.
Ethereal threads connect us all,
Inviting souls to rise and call.

Cosmic Resonance

In galaxies where echoes bloom,
A cosmic dance dispels the gloom.
With every pulse, the universe sings,
In waves of light, our spirit springs.

The stars align, a sacred tune,
In radiant hues, beneath the moon.
With every heartbeat, we connect,
In cosmic resonance, we reflect.

Ancient whispers fill the void,
In unity, our fears destroyed.
Each note we share, a bond divine,
In cosmic rhythm, our souls entwine.

Through stardust paths, we find our way,
In vibrant hues, we choose to stay.
With every touch, we feel the beat,
In cosmic resonance, our love's complete.

So hand in hand, we journey forth,
With every breath, we honor worth.
In timeless space, our spirits fly,
In cosmic resonance, we'll never die.

Shimmering Ascent

In whispered dreams, we dare to rise,
With every sigh, we touch the skies.
A shimmering path, our hearts ignite,
In boundless hope, we claim our light.

Through valleys deep and mountains tall,
We learn to rise, we learn to fall.
With every step, a story spun,
Shimmering ascent, our journey's begun.

The stars align, a guiding flame,
In courage found, we play the game.
With open hearts, we greet the sun,
Embracing all that we have won.

In unity, we chart our course,
Each challenge faced, a gentle force.
The tides may turn, but we stay strong,
In shimmering ascent, where we belong.

So let us soar, our spirits free,
Together bound, in harmony.
With every breath, our dreams take flight,
In shimmering ascent, we claim the night.

Celestial Chrysalis

In twilight's grace, the cosmos sleeps,
While secrets held, the silence keeps.
A spark of life, cocooned in night,
Emerging dreams, ignite the light.

With whispers soft, the stars converse,
In boundless skies, the universe.
From hidden depths, our spirits rise,
Celestial dance beneath the skies.

In tender threads of fate entwined,
Each flutter speaks, a truth defined.
In metamorphosis, we grow,
From chrysalis, our spirits flow.

The moon unveils the dawn's embrace,
Through cosmic trails, we find our place.
With every breath, in love we trust,
In celestial grace, we turn to dust.

So let the night unfurl its wings,
As harmony in starlight sings.
With open hearts, we claim our flight,
From shadows deep, to purest light.

Radiant Evolution

In morning's glow, the world awakes,
A vibrant shift, a dance that shakes.
Colors merge in a vivid blaze,
Life unfurls in wondrous ways.

The river flows with laughter bright,
As nature shifts from dark to light.
Petals open, reaching high,
To catch the whisper of the sky.

From seed to bloom, a journey grand,
Each moment joined by fate's own hand.
The dance of time, a sacred tune,
In every heart, a budding rune.

From shadows deep to radiant beams,
A cycle spins, with endless dreams.
Embrace the change, let beauty rise,
As life unfolds beneath the skies.

Constellations Unraveled

In skies above, the stars collide,
A tapestry where dreams abide.
Each constellation tells a tale,
Of ancient journeys, lost in veil.

The night unveils its secrets deep,
As starlit whispers start to creep.
Galaxies twist in cosmic dance,
While stardust weaves a fleeting chance.

A map of souls, in silver drawn,
Each twinkle speaks of hopes reborn.
Through distant worlds, our hearts can soar,
Unraveled paths to ancient lore.

Where wishes blend with cosmic streams,
And starlit visions fill our dreams.
In every glance towards that height,
We find our place within the night.

The Starry Metamorphosis

In cosmic realms, the night unfolds,
A canvas stretched, with tales untold.
Stars emerge from velvet black,
Transforming dreams, no turning back.

Each flicker hints at what could be,
A dance of light, a symphony.
The universe hums a soft refrain,
As constellations break their chain.

From silence born, a vibrant flare,
The void awakens with tender care.
The sky ignites in radiant hues,
As shadows fade, and hope renews.

In every twinkle, a story spun,
Metamorphosis has just begun.
By night's caress, our spirits rise,
Embracing change beneath the skies.

Shattered Moons

In the night's soft embrace,
Fragments of light dance,
Casting shadows on stones,
Whispers of stars' trance.

Broken dreams in the sky,
Echoes of what was whole,
Faded glimmers reply,
To the moon's silent role.

A tapestry of night,
Stitched with silver threads,
Each shard a tale of fright,
Of wishes left for dead.

Their brilliance remains bright,
In the hearts of the lost,
Guiding through darkened plight,
No matter the cost.

So we gather the shards,
To create what we seek,
In the universe's regard,
For the brave and the weak.

Echoes of Elysium

Amidst the golden fields,
Soft blooms start to sway,
Every petal reveals,
Whispers of lost play.

The air drenched in grace,
Where light kisses the ground,
Here time leaves no trace,
In joy, we are found.

Laughter drifts like song,
Carried by gentle breeze,
In a space where we belong,
Moments blend with ease.

Mirrors of the heart shine,
Reflecting what we seek,
In this realm divine,
Our spirits find their peak.

So let the echoes ring,
Through valleys of our fate,
For in this blossomed spring,
We learn to celebrate.

Cosmic Transitions

Stars burst into new forms,
Across the endless night,
Planets shift and transform,
Into brilliant light.

Celestial dance unfolds,
With gravity's embrace,
Stories from ages told,
In the vast cosmic space.

Nebulas weave a tale,
Of birth and silent death,
In the void, dreams sail,
Creating with each breath.

Infinite journeys start,
On comets made of ice,
Where stardust plays its part,
A tapestry of spice.

To the cosmos, we abide,
In transitions so grand,
With each star as our guide,
We embrace what is planned.

Orbiting Dreams

Planets spin in their dance,
Around a sun's warm glow,
Chasing dreams with each chance,
Through shadows, we flow.

Galaxies spin with grace,
Crafting paths in the night,
A dance through time and space,
In pursuit of the light.

Hopes collide like stars bright,
Creating novas of thrill,
In the dark, we ignite,
With visions to fulfill.

Orbiting worlds we chase,
Our dreams take us afar,
In this vast, endless place,
We reach for every star.

So we spiral around,
With love as our theme,
In the cosmos, we're found,
Awash in our dreams.

www.ingramcontent.com/pod-product-compliance
Ingram Content Group UK Ltd.
Pitfield, Milton Keynes, MK11 3LW, UK
UKHW021422230125
4262UKWH00028B/413

9 781805 617938